COMPOSER
SHOWCASE
HAL LEONARD
STUDENT PIANO LIBRARY

INTERMEDIATE LEVEL

Encantos Españoles
(Spanish Delights)

SIX PIECES FOR PIANO SOLO

BY EUGÉNIE ROCHEROLLE

D0613733

ISBN 978-1-4803-8295-4

CORPORATION

7777 W. BLUEMOUND RD. P.O. BOX 13819 MILWAUKEE, WI 53213

In Australia Contact:
Hal Leonard Australia Pty. Ltd.
4 Lentara Court
Cheltenham, Victoria, 3192 Australia
Email: ausadmin@halleonard.com.au

Visit Hal Leonard Online at
www.halleonard.com

Dedicated to Maria del Pico Taylor

CONTENTS

Alegrias

(Joyous Festival)

By Eugénie Rocherolle

Allegro (♩. = 69)

simile

To Coda ⊕

f

Añoranzas
(Yearnings)

By Eugénie Rocherolle

Mosso (♩ = 126)

subito *mf*

rit.

14

Las Señoritas

By Eugénie Rocherolle

Danza de Amor

By Eugénie Rocherolle

El Toreador

By Eugénie Rocherolle

(2nd time L.H. 8vb)

To Coda ⊕

_∧_ simile

Fiesta!

simile

THE EUGÉNIE ROCHEROLLE SERIES

Offering both original compositions and popular arrangements, these stunning collections are ideal for intermediate-level pianists! Each book includes a companion CD with recordings performed by Ms. Rocherolle.

Candlelight Christmas
Eight traditional carols: Away in a Manger • Coventry Carol • Joseph Dearest, Joseph Mine • O Holy Night (duet) • O Little Town of Bethlehem • Silent Night • The Sleep of the Infant Jesus • What Child Is This?
00311808..$14.99

Christmas Together
Six intermediate level piano duet arrangements: Blue Christmas • The Christmas Song (Chestnuts Roasting on an Open Fire) • Rudolph the Red-Nosed Reindeer • Santa Baby • Up on the Housetop • We Wish You a Merry Christmas.
00102838 ....$14.99

Classic Jazz Standards
Ten beloved tunes: Blue Skies • Georgia on My Mind • Isn't It Romantic? • Lazy River • The Nearness of You • On the Sunny Side of the Street • Stardust • Stormy Weather • and more.
00311424 ....$12.95

Continental Suite
Enjoy the wonders of Europe through these six original piano solos at the intermediate level: Belgian Lace • In Old Vienna • La Piazza • Les Avenues De Paris • Oktoberfest • Rondo Capichio.
00312111 ....$12.99

Disney Classics
Nine classic Disney songs as intermediate piano solos: Beauty and the Beast • Bibbidi-Bobbidi-Boo • Chim Chim Cher-ee • A Dream Is a Wish Your Heart Makes • It's a Small World • Mickey Mouse March • Supercalifragilisticexpialidocious • A Whole New World • Zip-A-Dee-Doo-Dah.
00312272 ....$14.99

It's Me, O Lord
Nine traditional spirituals: Deep River • It's Me, O Lord • Nobody Knows De Trouble I See • Swing Low, Sweet Chariot • and more.
00311368..$12.95

On the Jazzy Side
Six delightful jazz piano solos composed by Rocherolle, with her recordings of each on the enclosed CD! Songs: High Five! • Jubilation! • Prime Time • Small Talk • Small Town Blues • Travelin' Light.
00311982..$12.99

Recuerdos Hispanicos
Seven original solos: Brisas Isleñas (Island Breezes) • Dia de Fiesta (Holiday) • Un Amor Quebrado (A Lost Love) • Resonancias de España (Echoes of Spain) • Niña Bonita (Pretty Girl) • Fantasia del Mambo (Mambo Fantasy) • Cuentos del Matador (Tales of the Matador).
00311369..$12.95

Rodgers & Hammerstein
Selected Favorites
Exquisite, intermediate-level piano solo arrangements of eight favorites from these beloved composers: Climb Ev'ry Mountain • Do-Re-Mi • If I Loved You • Oklahoma • Shall We Dance? • Some Enchanted Evening • There Is Nothin' like a Dame • You'll Never Walk Alone. Includes a CD of Eugénie performing each song.
00311928..$14.99

Swingin' the Blues
Six blues originals: Back Street Blues • Big Shot Blues • Easy Walkin' Blues • Hometown Blues • Late Night Blues • Two-Way Blues.
00311445..$12.95

Two's Company
Eugénie Rocherolle gives us a charming and whimsical collection of five original piano duets written for the intermediate-level pianist. The CD includes a recording by Rocherolle of the duet, primo and secondo tracks allowing the performer to practice along with the CD. Duets include: Island Holiday • La Danza • Mood in Blue • Postcript • Whimsical Waltz.
00311883 ....$12.99

Valses Sentimentales
Seven original solos: Bal Masque (Masked Ball) • Jardin de Thé (Tea Garden) • Le Long du Boulevard (Along the Boulevard) • Marché aux Fleurs (Flower Market) • Nuit sans Etoiles (Night Without Stars) • Palais Royale (Royal Palace) • Promenade á Deux (Strolling Together).
00311497 ....$12.95

HAL•LEONARD®

www.halleonard.com

0513

COMPOSER SHOWCASE
HAL LEONARD STUDENT PIANO LIBRARY

This series showcases great original piano music from our **Hal Leonard Student Piano Library** family of composers, including Bill Boyd, Phillip Keveren, Carol Klose, Jennifer Linn, Mona Rejino, Eugénie Rocherolle and more. Carefully graded for easy selection, each book contains gems that are certain to become tomorrow's classics!

BILL BOYD

JAZZ BITS (AND PIECES)
Early Intermediate Level
00290312 11 Solos........................$6.99

JAZZ DELIGHTS
Intermediate Level
00240435 11 Solos........................$7.99

JAZZ FEST
Intermediate Level
00240436 10 Solos........................$7.99

JAZZ PRELIMS
Early Elementary Level
00290032 12 Solos........................$6.99

JAZZ SKETCHES
Intermediate Level
00220001 8 Solos........................$6.99

JAZZ STARTERS
Elementary Level
00290425 10 Solos........................$6.99

JAZZ STARTERS II
Late Elementary Level
00290434 11 Solos........................$7.99

JAZZ STARTERS III
Late Elementary Level
00290465 12 Solos........................$7.99

THINK JAZZ!
Early Intermediate Level
00290417 Method Book....................$10.99

DEBORAH BRADY

PUPPY DOG TALES
Elementary Level
00296718 5 Solos........................$6.95

TONY CARAMIA

JAZZ MOODS
Intermediate Level
00296728 8 Solos........................$6.95

SUITE DREAMS
Intermediate Level
00296775 4 Solos........................$6.99

SONDRA CLARK

DAKOTA DAYS
Intermediate Level
00296521 5 Solos........................$6.95

FAVORITE CAROLS FOR TWO
Intermediate Level
00296530 5 Duets........................$7.99

FLORIDA FANTASY SUITE
Intermediate Level
00296766 3 Duets........................$7.95

ISLAND DELIGHTS
Intermediate Level
00296666 4 Solos........................$6.95

THREE ODD METERS
Intermediate Level
00296472 3 Duets........................$6.95

MATTHEW EDWARDS

CONCERTO FOR YOUNG PIANISTS
FOR 2 PIANOS, FOUR HANDS
Intermediate Level Book/CD
00296356 3 Movements $16.95

CONCERTO NO. 2 IN G MAJOR
FOR 2 PIANOS, 4 HANDS
Intermediate Level Book/CD
00296670 3 Movements....................$16.95

PHILLIP KEVEREN

MOUSE ON A MIRROR
Late Elementary Level
00296361 5 Solos........................$6.95

MUSICAL MOODS
Elementary/Late Elementary Level
00296714 7 Solos........................$5.95

ROMP!
A DIGITAL KEYBOARD ENSEMBLE FOR SIX PLAYERS
Intermediate Level
00296549 Book/CD........................$9.95

SHIFTY-EYED BLUES
Late Elementary Level
00296374 5 Solos........................$6.99

TEX-MEX REX
Late Elementary Level
00296353 6 Solos........................$5.95

CAROL KLOSE

CORAL REEF SUITE
Late Elementary Level
00296354 7 Solos........................$6.99

DESERT SUITE
Intermediate Level
00296667 6 Solos........................$7.99

FANCIFUL WALTZES
Early Intermediate Level
00296473 5 Solos........................$7.95

GARDEN TREASURES
Late Intermediate Level
00296787 5 Solos........................$7.99

ROMANTIC EXPRESSIONS
Intermediate/Late Intermediate Level
00296923 5 Solos........................$8.99

TRADITIONAL CAROLS FOR TWO
Late Elementary Level
00296557 5 Duets........................$7.99

WATERCOLOR MINIATURES
Early Intermediate Level
00296848 7 Solos........................$7.99

JENNIFER LINN

AMERICAN IMPRESSIONS
Intermediate Level
00296471 6 Solos........................$7.99

CHRISTMAS IMPRESSIONS
Intermediate Level
00296706 8 Solos........................$6.99

JUST PINK
Elementary Level
00296722 9 Solos........................$6.99

LES PETITES IMAGES
Late Elementary Level
00296664 7 Solos........................$7.99

LES PETITES IMPRESSIONS
Intermediate Level
00296355 6 Solos........................$7.99

REFLECTIONS
Late Intermediate Level
00296843 5 Solos........................$7.99

TALES OF MYSTERY
Intermediate Level
00296769 6 Solos........................$7.99

MONA REJINO

CIRCUS SUITE
Late Elementary Level
00296665 5 Solos........................$5.95

JUST FOR KIDS
Elementary Level
00296840 8 Solos........................$7.99

MERRY CHRISTMAS MEDLEYS
Intermediate Level
00296799 5 Solos........................$7.99

PORTRAITS IN STYLE
Early Intermediate Level
00296507 6 Solos........................$7.99

EUGÉNIE ROCHEROLLE

**ENCANTOS ESPAÑOLES
(SPANISH DELIGHTS)**
Intermediate Level
00125451 6 Solos........................$7.99

JAMBALAYA
FOR 2 PIANOS, 8 HANDS
Intermediate Level
00296654 Piano Ensemble................$9.99

JAMBALAYA
FOR 2 PIANOS, 4 HANDS
Intermediate Level
00296725 Piano Duo (2 Pianos)........$7.95

TOUR FOR TWO
Late Elementary Level
00296832 6 Duets........................$7.99

TREASURES
Late Elementary/Early Intermediate Level
00296924 7 Solos........................$8.99

CHRISTOS TSITSAROS

DANCES FROM AROUND THE WORLD
Early Intermediate Level
00296688 7 Solos........................$6.95

LYRIC BALLADS
Intermediate/Late Intermediate Level
00102404 6 Solos........................$8.99

POETIC MOMENTS
Intermediate Level
00296403 8 Solos........................$8.99

SONATINA HUMORESQUE
Late Intermediate Level
00296772 3 Movements $6.99

SONGS WITHOUT WORDS
Intermediate Level
00296506 9 Solos........................$7.95

THROUGHOUT THE YEAR
Late Elementary Level
00296723 12 Duets......................$6.95

ADDITIONAL COLLECTIONS

ALASKA SKETCHES
by Lynda Lybeck-Robinson
Early Intermediate Level
00119637 8 Solos........................$7.99

AMERICAN PORTRAITS
by Wendy Stevens
Intermediate Level
00296817 6 Solos........................$7.99

COUNTY RAGTIME FESTIVAL
by Fred Kern
Intermediate Level
00296882 7 Rags........................$7.99

PLAY THE BLUES!
by Luann Carman (Method Book)
Early Intermediate Level
00296357 10 Solos......................$8.99

For full descriptions and song lists for the books listed here, and to view a complete list of titles in this series, please visit our website at www.halleonard.com

HAL•LEONARD® CORPORATION

7777 W. BLUEMOUND RD. P.O. BOX 13819 MILWAUKEE, WI 53213

0214